West Sussex SMUGGLERS' PUBS

First published in Great Britain in 2022
Copyright © 2022 Terry Townsend

A CIP catalogue record for this book is available from the British Library.

ISBN: 978 0 85710 129 7

PiXZ Books
Halsgrove House, Ryelands Business Park,
Bagley Road, Wellington,
Somerset TA21 9PZ
Tel: 01823 653777
Fax: 01823 216796
email: sales@halsgrove.com

An imprint of Halstar Ltd, part of the Halsgrove group of companies. Information on all Halsgrove titles is available at: www.halsgrove.com

Printed and bound in India by Parksons Graphics

West Sussex SMUGGLERS' PUBS

Terry Townsend

To my wife Carol
For in every sense this is her book, too

Acknowledgements
Thanks to Brenda and Tony Stables
for their continued help and encouragement

Plus special thanks to:
Jan Trott, Sussex resident and history buff
for undertaking much additional research

Janet Pennington, Sussex Historian
and the volunteers at Steyning Museum

And not forgetting all the help from the management
and staff of the featured pubs and inns.

CONTENTS

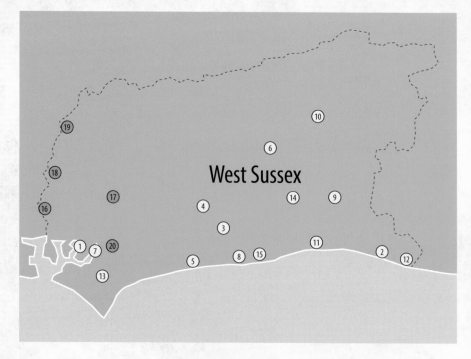

MAP KEY

The Pubs

1 Bosham, *The Anchor Bleu*
2 Brighton, *The Old Ship Hotel*
3 Burpham, *The George at Burpham*
4 Bury Common, *The Squire & Horse*
5 Climping, *The Black Horse*
6 Coolham, *The Selsey Arms*
7 Dell Quay, *Crown & Anchor*
8 Ferring, *The Tudor Close*
9 Fulking, *The Shepherd & Dog*
10 Lower Beeding, *The Crabtree Inn*
11 Old Shoreham, *The Red Lion*
12 Rottingdean, *The Black Horse*
13 Sidlesham, *The Crab & Lobster*
14 Steyning, *The Norfolk Arms*
15 West Tarring, *The George & Dragon*

Barbarous Usage Locations

16 Rowland's Castle
17 Charlton Forest
18 Lady Holt Park
19 Rake
20 Chichester:
   The Guildhall in Priory Park
   The Smugglers' Stone at the Broyle

INTRODUCTION

Through most of the past decade I have been engaged in writing a series of regional guide books tracing the smuggling history of English maritime counties from Cornwall to Suffolk. During this time I continued to consider the potential for West Sussex. Shoreham is the nearest harbour to London, the great magnet for contraband goods during the eighteenth century but I was concerned about the subsequent urban development of the seaboard from Bognor to Brighton. Would I be able to find enough clues to the smuggling past?

One of my early exploratory visits was to the village of Patcham near Brighton in search of The Black Lion, a former smugglers' haunt. I thought my fears had been confirmed when I discovered the building is now a suite of offices and I was directed to a new pub/hotel/eatery of the same name standing back from the busy A23 London to Brighton Road. Somewhat convinced of my original suspicion I wandered away from the traffic noise and headed back into the village to find the quiet church and churchyard of All Saints. I had read there was a smuggler's grave near the back of the church and I found it easily. The gravestone is inscribed:

DANIEL SKAYLES, Aged 34 Years
who was *unfortunately* shot:
on Thursday Evening
Nov 17th 1796.

The word 'unfortunately' appears in italics to emphasise the perceived injustice. The following verse originally appeared under the inscription but is now too weather-worn to decipher.

Alas! swift flew the fatal lead, Which pierced through the young man's head.

He instant fell, resigned his breath, And closed his languid eyes in death.

All you who do this stone draw near, Oh! pray let fall the pitying tear.

From this sad instance may we all Prepare to meet Jehovah's call.

The gravestone of smuggler Daniel Skayles in the churchyard of All Saints, Patcham.

Although exhorting passers-by to let fall a pitying tear on Daniel's behalf, there was no reference to the fact he lost his life whilst engaged in criminal activity. This omission is particularly telling because the majority of the population at that time did not regard smuggling as a crime.

Most people at the time considered the government responsible for the death of Daniel and others like him by engaging in a series of foreign wars and funding them by imposing extortionate import taxes and excise duties on a whole range of desirable goods.

By 1700 Britain was waging war in some part of the world well-nigh continuously against the forces of France, Holland and Spain. When Daniel was fourteen America was added to this list when Britain went to war against the colonists who had declared independence. Throughout Daniel's lifetime foreign war became an accepted way of life in these islands.

Right: Bo-Peep cottage was home to a Patcham smuggler and his family – perhaps even Daniel Skayles.

Other than the scant information on his gravestone we know little about Daniel's life but we know a vast amount about the world he was born into. Six years before his birth

A SHIP HAS BEEN SIGHTED
in this quarter
ENGAGING IN THE UNLAWFUL ACT OF

SMUGGLING

whosoever can lay information
leading to the capture of this ship
or its crew
will receive a reward of

£500

From His Majesty's Government.
This 19th day of October 1782

saw the start of the Seven Years' War – the war with France resulting in the imposition of higher taxes on tea and spirits providing the impetus for smuggling.

During the year he was born smuggling was already making an impact. Landowners were forced to raise farm labourers' wages to entice them out of service with smugglers and back to the land. One night's work on the beaches or along the smugglers' trails would earn a country labourer greater reward than a whole week's toil on the land.

The goods Daniel and his colleagues were transporting on that fateful night had been bought and paid for by shadowy English financiers including landowners, lawyers and even members of the aristocracy. French, Belgian and Dutch merchants had set up warehouses in maritime towns like Dunkirk, Ostend and Schiedam to supply English free traders with commodities including spirits, tobacco, tea and silks.

Smuggling gangs were protected by 'Batmen' bodyguards who could break a Preventive Officer's arm or crack his skull with their staves and clubs.

The *Sussex Weekly Advertiser*, the local newspaper of the time, contains a short report of the incident: 'One night last week, a desperate man named Leach, belonging to the Shoreham Custom-House boat, shot the servant of a smuggler through the head with a pistol. The deceased belonged to Patcham, and went by the name of Five-in-Nine.'

It was very common for members of smuggling gangs to adopt nicknames. Perhaps Daniel was one of a contingent of nine free traders from Patcham? It is also interesting to consider a smuggler having a servant; until you know the bailiff on nearby Stanmer Estate was one of the smuggling organisers and the estate chaplain was injured on his way back from a smuggling run. Someone with financial resources commissioned Daniel's gravestone.

An alternative account of the events of that unfortunate evening comes from eighteenth-century schoolmaster

Walter Gale of Mayfield. In his journal Gale describes Daniel as a 'desperate smuggler' travelling from Brighton as part of a large gang of men. The party encountered a patrol of Excise Officers and dragoons and proceeded to do battle with them. Excise Riding Officer Leach (no doubt with prize money on his mind) called out to Skayles, ordering him to release his 'booty'. When Daniel refused, the officer promptly shot him through the head.

Local tradition, says Daniel was actually pursued and shot after he emerged from one of the secret passageways

Southdown House Patcham, which stands opposite the original Black Lion, was built in 1711 with large cellars and metal latticework reinforcing the doors and shutters. There is still an escape tunnel linking the house with the former pub.

running between the cellars of houses and inns along the narrow Patcham High Street. Southdown House, which stands opposite the original Black Lion, was built in 1711 with large cellars and metal latticework reinforcing the doors and shutters. There is still an escape tunnel linking the house with the former pub.

On leaving All Saints' churchyard I noticed a neat cottage directly across the road and smiled when I saw the name 'Bo-Peep'; not because of the nursery rhyme but because of its hide-and-seek connotations with the local smuggling code. In an odd way Daniel became my inspiration for this journey and as things transpired I needn't have worried about finding evidence, there is much still to be seen.

DANIEL'S EXPERIENCE

On the 17th of November, or shortly prior to it, Daniel would have received instructions to meet with the gang at an agreed time and place where a landing was planned. Indeed, at the age of thirty-four, he might well have been one of the organisers of the run; all the more reason for him to be singled out by the zealous Leach.

On a typical smugglers' run, goods were shipped across the Channel at night in a 'lugger', often purpose-built for the task. The vessel would then wait off the English coast for a signal from a narrow beam of light cast from an oil lamp on shore. On seeing the signal, crew members hurriedly transferred the goods to a longboat for landing.

Piled high with half-anker casks of Boulogne brandy and large oilskin bags full of tea the long boat would be rowed swiftly through the surf to ground on shore where it was instantly hauled up the beach above the water-line. If Preventive men were patrolling in the area a warning

One night's contraband handling would earn a country labourer greater reward than a whole week's agricultural toil.

bonfire would be lit on a high point inland and the landing would be aborted for that night.

If the coast was clear and the longboat safely beached, anxious hands grabbed the heavy tea parcels and loaded them on the backs of waiting pack ponies and mules. The spirit casks, already roped together in pairs by the suppliers, were

French, Belgian and Dutch merchants set up warehouses in towns like Dunkirk, Ostend and Schiedam to supply English free traders with spirits, tobacco, tea and silks.

Right: On a typical smugglers' run, goods were shipped across the Channel in a 'lugger' and hurriedly transferred to a longboat for landing on beaches all along the West Sussex seaboard.

slung over the shoulders of 'tub-men' who were among the highest paid members of the gangs. These stalwarts were hired for their strength as they were required to carry two kegs at a time with a combined weight of approximately six stones (38kg). With one keg on their chest and a second on their back they headed off at a brisk pace over unsympathetic terrain such as sand dunes, marshes and slippery muddy tracks.

Within minutes of leaving the beach the lead section of the contraband convoy would be on the move, flanked by bodyguards known as 'bat-men' who wielded heavy staves or clubs. The first priority was to carry the goods inland to initial secure hiding places including barns, outhouses, hayricks, pigsties, cattle sheds, windmills, specially dug pits, churchyard tombs, church towers, church vestries and pub cellars.

Dating from the fifteenth-century, The Lion at Nytimber is happy to advertise its former role as a 'smugglers' haunt'.

THE SMUGGLERS' PUB

As you can imagine I often have my leg pulled about visiting so many pubs but a genuine smugglers' pub is the one place you can still get a sense of the desperate days of the free traders. Coincidentally, two other Black Lions I visited turned out to have impeccable smuggling histories. One is in nearby Rottingdean and the other at Climping, by the least spoilt section of the West Sussex coast.

In addition to supplying secret storage facilities the smugglers' pub served as a meeting place, recruitment

Violent skirmishes between Preventive Officers and smugglers often left dead or wounded.

Captain William James Mingaye of the Sussex coast blockade described The Royal George at Shoreham, under its landlady Mrs Anro as: 'nothing more than a pot house in a nest of smugglers'.

centre, distribution depot and valued customer. It was in the pubs that plots were hatched, arrangements for transportation agreed and runs commissioned. In all the southern counties of England the nerve centre of smuggling operations was predominantly the local ale house or pub. These wonderful old buildings with their low-beamed ceilings, flag stone floors, inglenook fireplaces and secret hiding places ooze history.

As you follow the pub trail in this book a fuller story of West Sussex smuggling will be revealed. Look particularly for a smuggler's spinner attached to a low beamed ceiling in some of the old bar rooms. Smugglers twirled these pointers to divide contraband spoils and wager some of their disposable income. It doesn't take much to imagine free traders like Daniel and his colleagues celebrating a successful run in one of these smoky candlelit rooms.

With a rowdy crowd of armed men in a heightened atmosphere with drink flowing it's easy to understand why the twisters were fixed to the ceiling where everybody could see and there could be no cheating. Variations on the spinners or twisters can still be seen today at The George at

Spirit casks, already roped together in pairs by the suppliers, were slung over the shoulders of 'tub-men' who headed off at a brisk pace over sand dunes, marshes and muddy tracks.

Smuggler's spinners or twisters, like this one at The Selsey Arms, Cooling, can still be seen mounted on the bar ceiling in a handful of West Sussex pubs.

Burpham, The Selsey Arms at Coolham, The Old Red Lion at Shoreham and the Spotted Cow at Angmering.

I give you a toast to Black Horses, Red Lions, Green Dragons, Spotted Cows, Blue Anchors and free traders like Daniel Skayles. They are all part of England's incredibly rich smuggling heritage.

THE PUBS

BOSHAM

The Anchor Bleu

High Street, Old Bosham PO18 8LS

Tel: 01243 573956

www.anchorbleu.co.uk

Bosham (pronounced 'Bozzum') is a gem of a place with a green at the very water's edge. As well as being popular with artists and the yachting fraternity it also attracts visitors interested in England's early history. The ancient church is depicted on the Bayeux Tapestry and Bosham is said to be the place where, in the twelfth century, King Canute demonstrated he had no control over the incoming tide. The misrepresented King is often described as being deluded about his own importance but his message was actually ironic. He was trying to show his fawning courtiers that his secular power was vain compared to the supreme

The Anchor Bleu is a traditional, family run pub in the historic and picturesque heart of Bosham.

The pub with its harbourside terrace can be seen in the background, to the right of the picture.

The rear patio is virtually on the waterfront at high tide, when it is inadvisable to park on the nearby beach!

power of God. It is also suggested a skeleton found during renovation work in the church in 1865 is that of Canute's daughter Gunhilda who is said to have drowned in Bosham Mill Stream.

From medieval times the government designated certain market towns and ports to be recognised as 'staple ports', where wool, hides of beasts, wine, corn or grain, and other

exotic or foreign merchandise could be transferred, carried or conveyed to be sold. The system was designed to make it easy for local and regional governments to monitor overseas trade and levy taxes to derive income and revenue.

Chichester was for centuries one of these privileged towns whose trade was handled through small 'outports' including Bosham, Dell Quay and later Emsworth. Where there are taxes there is inevitably tax evasion and alongside the legally sanctioned trade there was extensive smuggling. Bosham was regularly used by free traders who landed contraband at Bosham Hoe and carried it up to the village along a woodland track still known as 'Smugglers' Lane'.

Left: At high tide water laps at the defensive garden walls and submerges any cars left by people who have not seen or not heeded the warning notices.

Right: There is a worn flagstone floor in the dimly lit bar where beer pump handles reflect in the burnished brass counter.

When the summer has passed twin fireplaces warm the two cosy dining areas.

Left: At the back of the pub a foot-thick bulkhead door opens onto the delightful waterside terrace.

Right: Bosham was regularly used by free traders who landed contraband at Bosham Hoe and carried it up to the village along a woodland track still known as 'Smugglers' Lane'.

The Anchor Bleu is a traditional, family-run waterside pub located in the picturesque heart of Bosham. Stepping down into the dimly lit interior is to step back in time. People were generally much shorter in the days when smuggling was rife so now anyone much over 6 feet tall will find they are brushing their head on the bulging ochre-coloured beamed ceiling. There are two simple bars with worn flagstone floors. Beer pump handles are reflected in the burnished brass counter top and when summer has passed twin fireplaces warm the two cosy dining areas. There are up to six real ales and a good selection of popular sensibly-priced bar food.

During the free trading era 'neighbourhood watch' meant keeping an eye out for the Preventive men.

The charming terrace with lovely views over the sheltered inlet is virtually on the waterfront at high tide. It is accessed from one of the small dining rooms through a massive wheel-operated bulkhead door. Most of Bosham's pretty High Street backs onto the tidal creek and at high tide water laps at the defensive garden walls and submerges any cars left by owners who have not seen or not heeded the warning notices.

BRIGHTON
The Old Ship Hotel

Kings Road, Brighton BN1 1NR

Tel: 01273 329001

www.thehotelcollection.co.uk

The Old Ship's imposing exterior is a landmark of Brighton's seafront.

During the Regency era Brighton grew from the small fishing village of Brighthelmston to become the most fashionable town in Sussex and the biggest watering place in England, creating a high demand for smuggled luxuries. A visitor to Brighthelmston in the eighteenth century described the poverty-stricken inhabitants as: 'very needy and wretched, but skilled in nautical pursuits and in cheating the Customs men'.

Today the winding alleys and narrow courtyards known as 'The Lanes' remain much as they were in the eighteenth century when goods were landed on the beach and carried straight up into the old town for sale and distribution from a crowded complex of shops and inns.

The first record of a hotel on the site of The Old Ship comes from Tudor times. In 1559 a cottage belonging to Richard and

Today The Old Ship successfully combines modern design with many of the building's original period features.

Left: The site of the original inn can still be seen behind the present day entrance of 'The Old Ship Rooms'.

Right: In 1650 another hostelry opened on the opposite side of the broad cobbled street calling itself 'The New Ship Inn' (now Hotel du Vin).

John Gillham, in what is now Ship Street, is recorded trading as the Shippe Inn. The site of the original inn can still be seen behind the present day entrance of 'The Old Ship Rooms'. In 1650 another hostelry opened on the opposite side of the broad cobbled street calling itself 'The New Ship Inn' (now Hotel du Vin). From that time the original hostelry became known as The Old Ship Inn.

In 1671 The Old Ship was purchased by Captain Nicholas Tettersell with money given to him by King Charles II. Tettersell went on to become High Constable of Brighton. His successors extended the original inn by purchasing

adjacent Tudor buildings and extending house by house along Ship Street towards the sea.

The first two houses (today incorporating bedrooms 157 and 153) were linked to The Old Ship Inn by a stone spiral staircase that still sits within the present hotel. In the eighteenth century these unusual houses were occupied by two sisters who lived separately but shared the stairs.

In 1703 a great storm hit the town, sweeping away thirteen shops and cottages at the bottom of Ship Street leaving The Old Ship in the prominent seafront location it enjoys today.

A subterranean bar and dining room can be booked for functions offering a unique opportunity to explore the smugglers' tunnels.

The Smuggling History

In 1794 Preventive Officers investigating a commotion on Brighton beach discovered a gang of smugglers engaged in landing a huge cache of contraband goods. They summoned help from troops stationed nearby and successfully dispersed the free traders whilst also seizing 4500 kegs of gin.

In a typical scenario of the time two of the soldiers breached one of the kegs destined for the custom house and drank themselves insensible. They were found comatose on the beach the following morning. One, who was due to be married that day, was quite literally dead drunk and never recovered. This recurring problem arose because smuggled spirits were shipped 'over proof' to save cargo space and lessen transportation quantities. The fiery spirits were later reduced by adding water before delivery to the customer, much like pure drugs are cut today before supply.

The day of George IV's Coronation in 1821 presented a situation for smuggling opportunism. While the town celebrated elsewhere, free traders took advantage of the deserted streets and, completely unobserved, moved tubs of spirits from their temporary hiding place in The Old Ship's stables.

Contraband landed on the beach was carried straight up into the old town for sale and distribution in ancient pubs like The Black Lion and The Cricketers.

The Old Ship's imposing exterior is a landmark of Brighton's seafront and many of the individually designed bedrooms enjoy stunning sea views. Today the historic hostelry successfully combines modern design with many of the building's original period features. A subterranean bar and dining room can be booked for functions offering a unique opportunity to explore the labyrinth of smugglers' tunnels.

BURPHAM
The George at Burpham

Main Street BN18 9RR

Tel: 01903 883131

www.georgeatburpham.co.uk

Beginning life as a cottage in the eighteenth century The George opened as a pub around 1740.

The Old Saxon village of Burpham is tucked away down a long no through road with superb views over the Arun Valley to the mighty Arundel Castle. Standing across from the pub is the mainly twelfth- and thirteenth-century church of St Mary which was sensitively restored in the nineteenth century.

Reverend Robert Foster was curate here in 1845, towards the very end of the smuggling era. In 1850 he was appointed vicar and has left notes on the history of the village including this acknowledgement of Burpham's smuggling past: 'The double cottage just below Miss Harrison's is said to have been the oldest cottage in the parish and one of the oldest that his Grace has any title deeds of. It was said to have been the Burpham Inn & to have had cellars under it. Without doubt filled at times with smuggled spirits for they used to have loads at times through the village. Once only since my

holding have they as far as I know had a run through Burpham & then successfully'.

Miss Harrison's 'cottage' is actually a huge old house with an ancient interior, hidden behind a later Victorian frontage. It can be found on the same side as the church as the road slopes downhill towards Wepham and stands just before a brick and flint building with buttresses. Brandy and silks landed at Littlehampton were shipped up the river to the

Left: There are four hand pumps serving local ales including some from the Arundel Brewery just a few miles down the road.

Right: Saved from possible closure by local residents this historic pub was tastefully renovated and reopened in 2013 as The George at Burpham.

There is a dart board, and some games to play including a link to the past with the 'smugglers' spinner' still fixed to the ceiling.

foot of the 'Jacob's Ladder' path and then carried up the steeply rising track (known locally as 'Seventy Steps') into the heart of the village.

There has been no greater champion of Sussex pubs and Sussex ale than writer and poet Hilaire Belloc. In 1902, seeing the county he loved facing vast changes, he set off on a nostalgic walk from Robertsbridge on the Kent border journeying west to South Harting. A decade later he published his reflections in *The Four Men* which intriguingly suggest four facets of his own personality. Twenty-five years ago Bob Copper from the famous Sussex folk singing family retraced Belloc's steps across a landscape he already knew well. Bob published *Across Sussex with Belloc – In the Footsteps of 'The Four Men'*, which reads as a love letter to the county and its pubs. Reflecting on his youth he writes:

'In summer we walked up the river path to the George & Dragon at Burpham. Here, Ada West, the charming and

Contraband was stored in the copious cellars of Miss Harrison's 'cottage', which is actually a huge old house with an ancient interior, hidden behind a later Victorian frontage.

gracious landlady with a tremendous goitre, served ale in quart pots and told us of the days when, as a small girl in the 1860s, she used to help her parents serve up over sixty pints of beer every midday to the navvies who were laying the railway through the Arun Valley'.

The George at Burpham is a characterful old hostelry located at the heart of the village. Beginning life as a cottage in the eighteenth century it opened as a pub around 1740. Until recently this charming pub restaurant was known as The George & Dragon. Saved from possible closure by local residents it was tastefully renovated and reopened in 2013 as The George at Burpham.

The front part of this ancient freehouse is a proper bar with old pale flagstones and on the right a woodburning stove standing in a big inglenook. There are four hand pumps serving local ales including some from the Arundel Brewery just a few miles down the road. There is a carpeted area with nice scrubbed trestle tables and bar stools along the counter. A couple of tables share a small light flagstoned middle section with a big blackboard listing changing dishes. The George enjoys a well-deserved reputation for serving up excellent food.

The extended back area includes a light airy dining room leading to the garden with picnic sets and parasols. There is a dart board, and other games to play including a link to the past with the smugglers' spinner jenny still fixed to the ceiling.

Brandy and silks landed at Littlehampton were shipped along the river and carried up the 'Seventy Steps' into the heart of the village.

The George is the starting point for a network of local walks with old smugglers' trails leading right from the doorstep providing excellent riverside and downland rambles and, as you might expect, walkers and their dogs are welcome in the bar. The car park behind the pub is shared with the recreation ground which also has great views across the Arun Valley.

BURY COMMON
The Squire & Horse
Bury Common, Pulborough RH20 1NS
Tel: 01798 831343

Bury is one of the sleepier Sussex villages where neighbouring thatched cottages set amid colourful flower gardens populate the narrow winding lanes. This peaceful hamlet sits happily below the mighty Bury Hill from where spectacular views of the Arun Valley can be enjoyed. The river winds its course through a wide plain before finding its way to the edge of Bury. For many years a rowing boat ferry operated from the east bank for foot passengers bound for Amberley. Bob Copper remembered shouting across to old Bob Dudden the ferryman who was sawing logs in the garden of his cottage on the opposite side:

This lovely cottage is still known as The Black Dog & Duck. The half-timbered section to the rear was originally the village alehouse and haunt of smugglers.

'But we shouted in vain until at last the log dropped to the ground. Then, straightening his back and lighting his pipe, all the while effecting not to have heard our call, he presently looked up with feigned surprise, walked leisurely to the

wooden steps on his side of the water, untied the painter of his punt and slowly paddled across to pick us up'.

Bob explains it was all a charade played out with good humoured grace and the ferryman resolutely refused to take more than the two old fashioned brown pennies he diffidently asked for: 'In the course of less than ten minutes, in his quiet, unhurried way, he had firmly knocked on the head two of the commonest of human weaknesses – impatience and avarice.'

Bury has association with John Galsworthy whose best known work is The *Forsyte Saga*. Towards the end of his life the celebrated author lived in the Edwardian mansion called Bury House. This impressive Tudor-style building, now home to Manor House School, can be found in The Street, a little way down from The Squire & Horse.

Information about Bury smugglers has come down to us through the reminiscences of a Mrs Burchall who was born

The Squire & Horse stands back from the A29 next to the junction with 'The Street' which leads down into the village.

The Squire & Horse as the smugglers would have known it in the days before motorised traffic.

in the village in 1888. As a young girl she used to sit by the family fireside with her grandfather while he told her tales of local smugglers. When he was a lad he kept a look out for law officers and if possible distracted their attention when there was a run of goods being brought up from Selsey and Chichester Harbour.

The anxious local free traders were always on the lookout for excise 'runners' who were quite often close on their heels

This sizeable roadside dining pub has well-kept Harveys on draught plus a guest ale and a good choice of wines.

The comfortable interior has several partly divided beamed areas with country fireplaces throughout.

The U-shaped open plan bar has plush wall seats and is decorated with hunting prints and ornaments.

as they led their heavily laden pack ponies inland over the hills. Some goods were destined for West Burton and others to Bury where they were delivered to the Manor House. As a young girl Mrs B. and her friends were always told not to mention the Lord of the Manor by name.

There was a cave in an orchard where the smugglers stashed goods. A second entrance came out into The Manor House gardens from where they were taken into the house. One night when a group of smugglers was being pursued by excise men they didn't have time to get to the cave so escaped through Bury churchyard hastily dropping the contraband into a recently dug grave covering it quickly with the freshly dug earth. The parish church of St John the Evangelist lies east of the village centre on the river's west bank and is dominated by a twelfth-century tower surmounted by a cedar-shingled spire. The harassed men ran into the church hiding in the belfry until the excise men left.

When the coast was clear the gang transferred the contraband from the grave into the safety of the garden cave. Mrs Burchall said: 'The Lord the Manor disposed of the goods amongst his friends and grandfather had a bottle

The attractively presented food served in the flourishing two-level restaurant is freshly cooked to order and sourced locally wherever possible.

of rum for his part. He knew the village constable well and if the officers of the law came knocking on his door he'd hide his rum or brandy under Granny's skirt until they'd gone. The booty in question included lace, silk, brandy and tobacco – all of which was not heavy stuff.'

Standing back from the road junction in the heart of the village is the former Black Dog & Duck. Now a private home this old alehouse had been a centre for smuggling and was remembered by Bob Copper:

'Up in the village of Bury, where the sign of The Black Dog swings in the branches of a huge walnut tree we sat in a circle of friends and listened while they told us of illicit swan suppers to mark the end of the cricket season; and of the mead with a kick like a donkey made by a local farmer.'

There are lovely countryside views from the attractive patio garden.

The rear garden of Manor House School formerly featured a contraband cave.

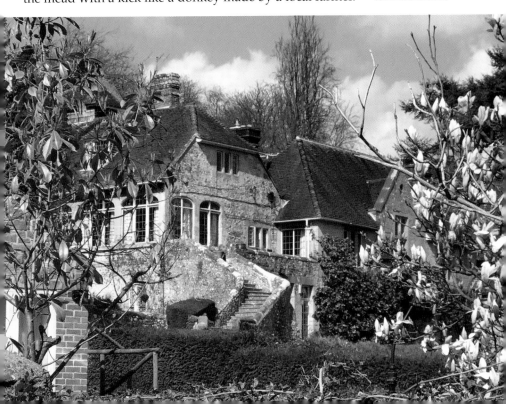

At the time Bob was a Worthing police constable and had come to the village to check on farm registers. He sampled the local mead and had to sleep off the effects under a haystack. Bob also explains how the pub got its unusual name:

'It was originally known as The Black Dog, and the sign bore a picture of Jim, a black retriever, who belonged to Mr Henly, the landlord. They were inseparable companions and were so frequently seen coming off the Brooks, he with a gun over his arm and Jim with a mallard in his jaws, that someone suggested that a duck should be added to the sign as you seldom saw one without the other.'

One night smugglers escaped through Bury churchyard dropping the contraband into a recently dug grave.

On one occasion, according to Mrs Burchall's grandfather, two lads from the village who had been drinking in the pub dressed up as ghosts and pranced up and down in the churchyard, to scare the excise men away.

The locals had codes to alert the smugglers when law officers were sniffing around. In the best tradition of 'Brandy for the Parson', both the vicar and the parish clerk were rewarded for their complicity with some spirits and tobacco which she said was hidden on coal and coke barges bringing fuel up to the village from 'Blighty' (Brighton). Mrs Burchall was born in 1888 and her parents died in 1930. She talks about cottage rents of 7d a week being paid to The Duke of Norfolk's estate and it seems likely, although living in Arundel Castle, he was the said Lord of The Manor of Bury.

Was Bernard Howard (12th Duke of Norfolk), the Lord of the Manor who Mrs Burchall and her friends were told never to mention by name?

On Yeakall & Gardner's map of 1783 the main road turns into 'The Street' and continues through the centre of Bury. Standing back from the junction is The Squire & Horse, a sizeable roadside dining pub, built in the sixteenth century and extended a few years ago. By 1813 a bypass had been constructed which is the present day A29.

Originally known as 'The White Horse', this welcoming old pub was frequented by smugglers and Preventive men. It has several partly divided beamed areas with country fireplaces throughout. The U-shaped open-plan bar has plush wall seats and is decorated with hunting prints and ornaments. The attractively presented food served in the flourishing two-level restaurant is freshly cooked to order and sourced locally wherever possible. They have well-kept Harveys on draught plus a guest ale and a good choice of wines.

CLIMPING
The Black Horse

Climping Street, Littlehampton BN17 5RL

Tel: 01903 715175

The eighteenth-century Black Horse Inn could be nothing less than a well-established smugglers' rendezvous.

The beautiful village of Climping attracts more than its share of visitors on summer days. The lovely church of St Mary is a gem, full of interest. An antiquary once used the phrase: 'Bosham for antiquity, Boxgrove for beauty and Climping for perfection'. In addition Climping enjoys almost the only stretch of shoreline in West Sussex which still remains undeveloped and consequently conveys something of the character and atmosphere the free traders would have known. Located between Littlehampton and Middleton, Climping Beach has a straggling line of trees backing the shore and the impression of the old smuggling days is heightened by a few old farm buildings.

The reason Climping enjoys unspoilt serenity today is due to multi-millionaire Walter Guinness – 1st Baron Moyne, who in the early twentieth century, stopped a major housing

development of the type that has swamped the majority of the West Sussex seaboard. In protecting his decadent private hideaway of Bailiffscourt, Lord Moyne helped to create what has become known as 'Climping Gap', the largest open area of undeveloped coast between Brighton and Bognor Regis.

Bailiffscourt today is a beautiful contradiction. It is a prestigious hotel and spa complex comprising 39 luxurious bedrooms spread throughout the main house and cottages on the estate. The buildings are convincingly medieval but in fact are modern constructions built using architectural salvaged materials from the twelfth and thirteenth centuries. Examples include the main oak door of the 'New House' which is fifteenth-century and came from South Wanborough church. The arch itself was originally of Holditch Priory and an oak window once fronted a house near Muchelney Abbey.

The unspoilt Beach at Climping with its straggling line of trees backing the shore conveys something of the character and atmosphere the free traders would have known.

The impression of former smuggling days is heightened by a few old farm buildings standing back from the only stretch of shoreline in West Sussex which still remains undeveloped.

In 1745 4 or 5 tons of tea were landed here at Elmer from the smuggling cutter *Samuel Betts* of Rye. The thirty-six smugglers captured were all from West Sussex and some (if not all) would have frequented The Black Horse.

The Bailiffscourt Estate has recently acquired The Black Horse Inn, saving it from closure and an uncertain future. In this special location, the eighteenth-century hostelry could be nothing less than a well-established smugglers' rendezvous. It is said there was a smugglers' tunnel

linking The Black Horse to the church and an old tomb in the churchyard was reputedly used by smugglers to hide contraband landed nearby at Elmer Sluice. In 1745 4 or 5 tons of tea were landed at Elmer from the smuggling cutter *Samuel Betts* of Rye.

In 1825, during the Coast Blockade period, the station at East Elmer experienced a number of problems and desertions thought to be due to the harsh regime. On 8 April thirty new men arrived at Littlehampton to join nearby stations. Some were due to go to East Elmer replacing four men who had recently deserted.

Lieutenant Newman, a harsh disciplinarian, was replaced by Lieutenant James Carter. The new officer was soon involved

Bailiffscourt is a prestigious hotel and spa complex spread throughout buildings which are convincingly medieval but in fact are modern constructions built from architectural salvaged materials from the twelfth and thirteenth centuries.

It is said there was a smugglers' tunnel linking The Black Horse to the church and an old tomb in the churchyard was reputedly used by smugglers to hide contraband landed nearby at Elmer Sluice.

in a violent fight with smugglers when he shot dead local free trader Charles Horne. Next month Richard Harrison, one of the early deserters from East Elmer, met up with his old pal Sentinel Jim Sullivan and tried to persuade him to go for a drink in The Black Horse at Climping. Sullivan refused and told Lieutenant Carter who went to the inn and found the deserter playing skittles with a corporal and two lancers of the dragoons. Carter demanded the soldiers help in securing Harrison as a prisoner but, as they were not under the command of a Blockade Officer, the orders were ignored and the deserter slipped away again.

COOLHAM
The Selsey Arms

Coolham Crossroads, Coolham RH13 8QJ

Tel: 01403 741537

The Selsey Arms occupies a generous plot of land which would have been busy on the occasion of a smugglers' 'run' when the pub provided refreshment for the free traders and fodder for their mounts.

Writing before WW2 Arthur Mee said of Coolham: 'It is on the map, but that is all; it lies far from anywhere, down lanes in a hidden corner of the Sussex Weald'. Mee could have been describing the Coolham of a century or so earlier when it was a perfect resting place for free traders and their horses engaged in transporting untaxed goods from the coast up through the important market town of Horsham. Although the population was scattered, this former hotbed of smuggling, had a village 'Club' with enough support to march with between 200 and 300 members and friends to an annual dinner in a 90 feet long marquee.

Today this old smugglers' haunt is no longer hidden because it stands at a crossroads busy with passing traffic. Although the quiet lanes described by Mee are now just a memory the pub itself still has breathing space around it which is given over to gardens and car parking.

Today the pub fronts the junction of the B2149 and the A272. During the smuggling era both roads were quiet country lanes.

When I called the pub was run by friendly landlord Kenny Easton and his wife Belinda who serve a great pint of Harveys.

The Pub

The original pub the smugglers frequented, is incorporated into the southeast corner of the present day building. It is a seventeenth-century timber framed cottage with red brick infilling, partly refaced with brick and tarred weatherboarding. It was formerly known as The Duke's Head and before that The King of Prussia. The last major changes to the interior were made in the 1950s when it was opened out to a three room layout.

The Selsey Arms is a comfortable, traditional country pub serving Harveys Sussex, Sharp's Doom Bar and Flowers IPA. Wooden floors, exposed brickwork, three fireplaces and a 'smugglers' spinner' affixed to the bar ceiling all help to retain the feeling of days gone by.

Belinda happily confirming The Selsey Arms is the most dog friendly of pubs.

All the food is home-cooked and one room of this otherwise informal village hostelry, has a slightly more restaurant feel. It is decorated as a tribute to the squadron of Polish airmen who used the pub when stationed at Coolham airfield

Wooden floors, exposed brickwork, three fireplaces and a 'smugglers' spinner' affixed to the bar ceiling all help to retain the feeling of days gone by.

49

GENTLEMENS TOI

Left: When Kenny was looking for somewhere to place his CCTV screen he discovered this antique roasting 'spit wheel'.

Right: In earlier times small dogs were used to drive wheels which were linked by a chain to a spit over the open fire.

during the Battle of Britain. The names of fifteen of these men who died defending our freedom are inscribed in gold lettering on three Scottish polished black granite tablets set into the locally quarried West Sussex stone of the pub's front garden wall.

The lower bar area is carpeted and has an open log fire. Above and to the right of the fireplace is a small monitor screen relaying CCTV pictures from a bird nesting box in the garden. When landlord Kenny Easton was looking for somewhere to place the screen he uncovered an antique roasting 'spit wheel' set into the wall to the right of the chimney breast. In earlier times small dogs were used to drive these wheels which were linked by a chain to a spit over the open fire.

The dining room is decorated as a tribute to a squadron of Polish airmen who used the pub when stationed at Coolham airfield during the Battle of Britain.

A feature of the rear garden is a stream-side decking area with tables and parasols.

The former stables have been converted to provide two comfortable *en suite* bedrooms.

Among the old photographs displayed on the bar walls is one of the former windmill at Baileys Farm, Coolham. It originally stood at Kirdford, where it was erected between 1770 and 1780 and was moved to Coolham around 1800. Enterprising local smugglers created an ingenious storage space for contraband behind the mill wheel.

This old photograph in the bar shows the local windmill where enterprising smugglers created an ingenious storage space for contraband behind the mill wheel.

The pub's front garden borders the roadside but the attractive rear garden is more secluded. A river runs along the bottom boundary where there is a stream-side decking area with tables and parasols to maximise this pleasant feature. Accommodation is also provided in four *en suite* rooms, two of which are located in the converted stables where contraband was formerly stored.

DELL QUAY

Crown & Anchor

Dell Quay Road, Apuldram, Chichester PO20 7EE

Tel: 01243 781712

The modernised fifteenth-century Crown & Anchor occupies a splendid spot on the ancient Quay overlooking Chichester Harbour.

Goods have been imported and exported, legally and illegally, through Dell Quay on Chichester Harbour for more than 2,000 years. It was the smallest and oldest port in Sussex and from Roman times the official landing stage for all goods coming into Chichester Harbour. It is possible the Roman Road 'Stane Street', which entered the ancient settlement of Noviomagus Reginorum (Chichester) through the east gate linking the city with London, also went southwards to the Manhood Peninsula via Dell Quay.

The original port stood about half-a-mile west of Apuldram Church moving to its present site in the seventeenth century.

Left: The comfortable bow-windowed lounge bar provides extensive views across the harbour.

Right: Summer visitors can enjoy the marine vistas from terrace picnic sets.

The name Dell means a deep hollow or depression, which probably referred to the eastern arm of the Chichester Channel. During the Medieval period Dell Quay was the wool port of Chichester and seventh most important port in the country. At that time its foreign imports included Spanish wine, Irish provisions such as timber, barley and coal plus building stone from quarries on the Isle of Wight. In 1587, during the Reign of Elizabeth I, three vessels equipped by the merchants of Chichester and mainly manned by seamen from the city, sailed to fight the Spanish Armada.

During the eighteenth and early nineteenth century when smuggling was rife, the Quay had its full share of contraband cargoes. There can hardly have been a day when smuggling was not discussed or planned over a mug of Sussex ale or tot of brandy under the roof of the Crown & Anchor. On the infrequent occasions when the authorities managed to seize a cache, Chichester Customs House would place a sales advertisement in the local paper. Typical is this example which appeared in *The Hampshire Chronicle and Chichester Journal* on 7 June 1784 offering for sale by auction: '3220 gallons of brandy, 15 gallons of rum, 2332 gallons of Geneva and 1200 small empty casks'.

Another appearing on 23 August shows the broad range of goods being smuggled including: '794 gallons of brandy, 53

Popular dishes are available from the all-day servery.

gallons of rum, 516 gallons of Geneva, 5lbs of nutmeg, 57 yards of striped cotton, 8 wicker baskets, 119 pieces of china and earthenware. 13 pieces of Nankeen, 4 pairs of leather shoes, 2 pairs of leather slippers and 5 snuff boxes'. The goods were meant for sale to the public not trade, however local publicans used to send agents to the sales to bid surreptitiously on their behalf.

With a direct route to London, the resourcefulness of smugglers in the Quay particularly flourished around the

In winter the glow of two fires reflects off a wealth of beams.

There is a well-kept range of real ales.

beginning of the nineteenth century. Naturally there are many stories, one persistent unconfirmed rumour suggests there was a vicious fight between smugglers and Revenue men that took place in the Crown & Anchor. The smugglers were chased down into the 500 year old pub cellars where five of the King's men were killed. In addition the leader of the free traders was said to be the local vicar. A number of churchmen were known to take the side of their impoverished parishioners against what they saw as an unfair law.

Dell Quay continued to serve as the city's port until 1824 when the Chichester Canal was built from Birdham to a basin in the city providing a direct route from Portsmouth to the Yorkshire coast without going via the sea. The canal also went to the River Arun at Ford via Yapton. Even today a local person who does not properly close a door can be asked: 'Do you come from Yapton?' referring to the time when villagers used to leave their doors unlocked to enable fleeing smugglers to escape the Revenue men by running through the cottages.

There is no commercial trade at Dell Quay today and it is a pleasant place for small boat sailing, racing, walking and bird watching. The old warehouses are used by Dell Quay Sailing Club. The modernised fifteenth-century Crown & Anchor occupies a splendid spot on the Quay overlooking Chichester Harbour.

The former smugglers' den is very popular and best visited at high tide and quiet times. There is a panelled public bar and comfortable bow-windowed lounge bar with extensive views. Summer visitors can enjoy the terrace picnic sets. Dogs are welcome and there are good walks straight from the pub. In winter the glow of two open fires reflects off a wealth of beams. There is a well-kept range of real ales and popular dishes are available from the all-day servery.

Stories are still told of a vicious fight between smugglers and Revenue men that took place in The Crown & Anchor when five of the King's men were killed in the pub's 500 year old cellars.

Dating from the twelfth century, this striking thatched barn with flint walls now serves as the village pub.

FERRING

The Tudor Close

63 Ferringham Lane, Ferring, Worthing BN12 5NQ

Tel: 01903 243155

Historic Ferring maintains its village identity even though it is now part of the built-up area of Worthing. Accessed along the A259, it lies 3 miles west of the town with approximately equal size green buffers on either side and to the north the open parkland area of Highdown Hill.

All around Ferring there is evidence of the old smuggling days. In Ferring Street, Smuggler's Cottage and Annex were both used for contraband storage. Vine Cottage at 35 Ferring Street and Landalls at 37 both served a similar purpose, as did the building in Ferringham Lane now known as The Tudor Close Pub & Restaurant. Goods deposited in these hiding places were brought up from the beach along the small River Rife, which passes close by.

Ferring's major claim to smuggling fame, lies buried on Highdown Hill overlooking the village. John Oliver was an eccentric local miller who lived in a cottage he owned near to the mill which survived until 1826. He was a true eccentric and busied himself in his spare time constructing elaborate mechanical models. One of these creations attached to the roof of his house was animated by wind power and depicted an Excise man chasing a smuggler with an old woman hot on his heels laying about the officer with her broom. This image, together with the miller's wealth, has fuelled speculation that Oliver was involved in smuggling and some people believe he was the leader, or at least the financier of the local gang.

The greatest of the miller's eccentricities related to his anticipation of death. He made his own coffin and kept it in readiness under his bed. He also built his own tomb twenty-seven years before it was eventually required. This has led to speculation that in the interim it was used as a contraband store.

In the main dining/function room there is a remarkable fireplace with carved surround.

The Tudor Close is mentioned in the Doomsday Book. Today it enjoys a deserved reputation for its good food and friendly atmosphere.

The present day impressive interior has a high-beamed ceiling and a mezzanine gallery area.

When miller Oliver finally died in 1793 everything was ready with all the arrangements made long in advance. The funeral was a gay affair attended by 2000 brightly dressed people. His coffin was carried from the house to the tomb by pall bearers dressed in white and twelve-year-old Ann Street of Goring, read a sermon of the miller's choosing.

There is a local tradition that Oliver was buried face down, because he believed when the last judgment came the world would be turned topsy-turvy and he would be the only one facing right-side-up. The tomb, fenced round with metal railings, commands a prominent position in this downland setting. Nearby is Highdown Gardens, one of the hidden gems of the area and home to a unique collection of rare plants and trees.

They serve two regular beers, Fuller's London Pride and Sharp's Doom Bar plus three changing beers.

Contraband was also secreted at Landells, 37 Ferring Street, which marks the northern most point of the original settlement.

Miller Oliver's tomb stands on the summit of Highdown Hill. His cottage and windmill are long gone.

Previous, top: Contraband landed here on the beach at Ferring was initially secreted in The Tudor Close barn and in a number of village cottages.

Previous, bottom: Vine Cottage at 35 Ferring Street was used as a contraband store.

The Tudor Close is a striking, thatched building. Now serving as the village pub it enjoys a deserved reputation for its good food and friendly atmosphere. Mentioned in the Domesday Book, this old Sussex barn, with its flint walls dates from the twelfth century. During the early years the barn stood among fields leading to the seashore and in the eighteenth century it became an ideal location for smugglers to hide their untaxed goods. In later years it was used by farmers for storage of grain and fodder harvested from the

The chalk gardens at Highdown, home to a unique collection of rare plants and trees, are well worth a visit.

abundance of nearby crops and during WW2 was seconded as HQ for the French Canadian Air Force.

The present day impressive interior has a high beamed ceiling and a mezzanine gallery area. In the main dining/function room is a remarkable fireplace with carved surround. The conservatory covers the earlier pub courtyard, originally the old cow yard. They serve two regular beers, Fuller's London Pride and Sharp's Doom Bar plus three changing beers.

FULKING
The Shepherd & Dog

The Street, Henfield BN5 9LU

Tel: 01273 857382

The village of Fulking hides away in the dramatic up-along, down-along country to the west of Devil's Dyke. Its historic local pub, The Shepherd & Dog, shelters snug from the winds in a hollow of grassy high hills. For centuries sheep and Fulking were synonymous. Even at the beginning of the nineteenth century there were said to be 2600 sheep in the parish but only 258 people.

The aptly named Shepherd & Dog is situated in a picturesque location at the side of a steep lane leading down from the village.

It is a general misconception that the first large scale smuggling involved the importation of contraband alcohol and tobacco but in fact, for the greater part of its history, smuggling primarily involved the illicit export of wool.

HE SENDETH SPRINGS
INTO THE VALLEYS
WHICH RUN AMONG
THE HILLS
THAT MEN WOULD
PRAISE THE LORD
FOR HIS GOODNESS

Wool has played a central part in the economic history of England recognised today in the woolsack on which the Lord Speaker sits in the House of Lords.

The involvement of historic Marsh and Downland pubs in this commerce is reflected in names like The Fleece, The Woolpack, The Lamb and here at Fulking with The Shepherd & Dog where wool shorn from sheep outside the pub door was destined to be illegally exported through the port at Shoreham.

In May and June each year many other Downland villages sent their sheep to Fulking to be washed prior to the annual shearing. The spring of clear water which rises here was eminently suitable for the purpose. A dam was made to hold the stream, whilst the sheep were kept in readiness in a pen. The washing was carried out by two or three men who stood in the cold water for several hours. When the sheep washing was over for the day the men involved would walk stiff with cold and dripping with water the short distance to the pub to warm themselves by the impressive inglenook

Previous: The spring of clear water which rises by the pub's car park entrance was eminently suitable for annual sheep washing.

Downland sheep still graze on hills surrounding the pub. In former times many other local villages sent their sheep to Fulking to be washed prior to the May and June annual shearing.

The stream which today flows through the pub garden was dammed to hold the water whilst the sheep were kept in readiness in a pen.

fire. Rheumatism took its toll of these poorly paid heroes who normally could continue in this work for only a few years while illegal export of fleeces made fortunes for their land-owning employers.

Smugglers' Lane at Fulking is a reminder of the days when contraband imports from Shoreham passed north through the village *en route* for markets in London.

When the sheep washing was over for the day the men involved would walk stiff with cold and dripping with water the short distance to the pub to warm themselves by this impressive inglenook fire.

Good, locally sourced food is served daily in the traditional dining room.

Shoreham is the closest Sussex port to London and by the early nineteenth century contraband imports were passing north through Fulking, finding a temporary hiding place in a pit below The Shepherd & Dog. In 1844 Nathaniel Blacker the Waywarden for Fulking discussed the practice in 'Sussex in Bygone Days'. It seems the goods were first taken up the pub's exterior steps before being lowered through a concealed opening into a large cavity below which had been incorporated in structural changes made to the pub over time.

In 1927 a local newspaper reporter shown the cavity described it as a large chamber. An example of this kind of contraband pit can be seen today at The Lamb in Hooe, in East Sussex, where they have made a feature of it.

Situated in a picturesque location at the side of a steep lane leading down from the village this sizeable cottage-style pub with four-gabled attics has a welcoming unpretentious interior. The pub itself comprises a large traditionally-styled room with low beams and plenty of tables. Outside is a sunny patio area overlooking the lane. The small stream flowing through the spacious garden reminds us of the sheep shearing legacy.

The Shepherd & Dog is the main outlet for the excellent Downlands Brewery

The Shepherd & Dog is the main outlet for the excellent Downlands Brewery and at least three of their beers are usually available as well as a changing selection of guest ales. Good, locally sourced food is available daily. Walkers and dogs are welcome and the garden bar, available in good weather, is very popular during regular beer and cider festivals.

This photograph from the 1920s shows how little the outward appearance of the pub has changed.

Opposite: During the smuggling era the pub had a contraband hiding pit below the floor like this one at The Lamb in Hooe, East Sussex.

This family-run pub has a Victorian façade but is much older inside.

LOWER BEEDING

The Crabtree Inn

Brighton Road, Lower Beeding, Horsham RH13 6PT

Tel: 01403 892666

www.crabtreesussex.co.uk

Crabtree is a hamlet in the parish of Lower Beeding, situated on the busy A281 road five miles southeast of Horsham. The modern parish includes most of St Leonard's Forest which was a favoured smugglers' rendezvous.

On the morning of Sunday 6 December 1778 a band of 190 men, their horses laden with bags of tea and bales of cloth, rode through the main street of Henfield on a regular route north which took in The Crabtree Inn at Lower Beeding. This time the smugglers had seven captive Revenue Officers with them who were later released unharmed. These particular Preventive men were fortunate; some officers were killed in fights where they were always hopelessly outnumbered

whilst others were found dead after unexplained falls from cliff tops. More still were shipped over to France on smugglers' luggers and left to make their own way home back across the channel.

Contraband pack trains like this, heading north from Shoreham, were engaged in supplying luxuries to eager customers in local towns or delivering bulk consignments to

Left: The décor throughout is light and modern but there is evidence of Tudor beams.

Right: The main part of the building we see today is late eighteenth century but areas of the inn are 400 years old with this inglenook dating to 1537.

The food at The Crabtree is excellent and their selection of real ales, beer and wine is first class.

Today this historic Wealden barn with its hayloft door has been converted into a dining room but during the smuggling era there is no doubt it would have served to store contraband.

commercial distribution centres on the outskirts of London. It was all highly organised and with this number of men and horses staged refreshment points were an essential part of the plan. The Crabtree Inn between Cowfold and Lower Beeding was perfectly positioned to serve this function. In 1799 a party of hungry soldiers appeared at the inn seeking food. When told there was none one of them, presumably an officer, paid half a guinea for a caged canary, then had it killed and cooked.

This family run pub has a Victorian façade but is much older inside. The main part of the building we see today is late eighteenth century but areas of the inn are 400 years old. Inside there are Tudor beams and an inglenook dated to 1537. The décor throughout is light and modern.

At the rear are landscape gardens with a massive ancient yew tree and extensive westerly views across a heavily wooded valley. At the side of the paved terrace is an ancient Wealden barn with a hayloft door. Today this historic shiplap building has been converted into a dining room but during the smuggling era there is no doubt it would have served to store contraband.

The Crabtree was tastefully refurbished and re-opened as a family run restaurant and pub having been closed for a considerable period of time. The emphasis is on food. The lunch menu changes daily and the Sunday menu weekly. There is a restaurant, several private dining rooms and front and side bars. The food at The Crabtree is excellent and their selection of real ales, beer and wine can be enjoyed in the beautiful garden – weather permitting.

Left: Lower Beeding is dog walking country *par excellence* with the promise of refreshment in the lovely garden of The Crabtree Inn.

Right: There are extensive westerly views across a heavily-wooded valley from the landscaped gardens with its massive ancient yew tree, already centuries old when smugglers used to call here.

Drivers using the A281 today might find it hard to believe life in front of The Crabtree was ever this tranquil.

SHOREHAM by SEA
The Red Lion

Old Shoreham Road BN43 5TE

Tel: 01273 453171

Shoreham is the nearest Channel port to London and the great uninterrupted sweep of sand and shingle beaches stretching for almost 30 miles offered excellent opportunities for landing vast quantities of contraband. An official report from the late 1700s mentions three vessels at a time unloading at Shoreham and the area Excise Supervisor confessed he felt powerless to intervene against the armed convoys as the goods were transported inland.

The Red Lion was established in the sixteenth century in part of a former monastery and cottage. It is set below the present road level as the highway was raised since its origins as a village track.

The Red Lion was trading throughout the smuggling era and would have been a meeting place for local free traders like Thomas Vincent. One day in the 1820s, whilst quietly engaged in creeping up sunken tubs, Vincent was spotted by a blockade man. The smuggler said he had simply come across the brandy when fishing and put in a finders claim for a reward. His application however was rejected when another of his boats was captured soon after in Shoreham Harbour with silks and kid gloves on board.

Writing in 1927 author R. Thurston Hopkins included this entreaty in his *Sussex Pilgrimages*: 'If you should ever chance to be near the 'Red Lion' at Old Shoreham do not fail to pause for refreshment'. By the time of Hopkins visit in the 1920s the main road to Brighton had been realigned and ran immediately south of the inn. The pub was also set below the present road level as the highway had been raised since its origins as a village track. Although the interior has been opened up a little anyone visiting this old smugglers' haunt today would easily recognise it from Hopkins' description:

'Down some stone steps you walk into the parlour (or rather four or five box-like rooms which are very reminiscent of a doll's house) and find yourself in a very ancient abode. If any inn was a haunt of smugglers surely this was, for everything here seems to have a flavour of the sea. The dim cabin-like rooms seem to be still rich with the aroma of tar and rum, and the very floor is wavy like the sea and your feet seem to rock to the swell of the tide'.

The Red Lion stands opposite the end of the old timber bridge spanning the River Adur.

Convoys of farm carts like these were used to transport smuggled goods through Shoreham.

Massive oak beams support the ceiling in the present day bar which was the original part of the building.

The inn was established in the sixteenth century in part of a former monastery and cottage. It had been central to life in the old village for a couple of hundred years before it was extended and lengthened to the north and again in the nineteenth century to the south. By this time it had developed as a coaching inn serving the roads east towards Brighton and north along the bank of the River Adur towards Steyning.

Today the old inn is listed by English Heritage as a Grade II building for its architectural and historical importance; the latter being partly due to poet laureate Alfred Lord Tennyson. In the nineteenth century The Red Lion played a significant part in a locally famous tragedy which gained wider recognition when Tennyson wrote his poem, *Rizpah*, based on events which took place here.

The ubiquitous 'smugglers' spinner' is affixed to a beam in the low ceilinged bar.

On 1 November 1792, the driver of the local mail coach had to deliver a letter containing half a sovereign* on his usual route between Brighton and Shoreham. At Hove he was robbed by two Shoreham men, one of whom went on to The Red Lion to meet with drinking companions.

Phoebe Hessel, a well-known Brighton resident who frequented the inn, overheard the felon discussing the crime. She reported him to the local parish constable who arrested him and his young accomplice. The robbery had involved no violence but the men were sentenced to death at Horsham Assizes. They were tied to horses and transported under military and police escort.

On 26 April 1793 a large crowd watched as they were hanged at the scene of the crime and their corpses displayed

on a gibbet. The younger man's mother was so distraught that over time she travelled nightly to Hove to collect the decaying bones and flesh, eventually interring them in the graveyard at St Nicolas' church adjacent to the rear of The Red Lion.

Another bizarre event involving a dead robber occurred at the inn during the final years of the smuggling era. A man burgled several houses in Shoreham but when he broke into a local eighteenth-century mansion called Buckingham House** he was shot dead. Nobody could identify him so his body was placed in a glass-topped coffin and left at the inn in case any visitors recognised his face.

Hundreds of people travelled to Shoreham to inspect the coffin, but the man was eventually identified by his dog, which appeared at the inn, saw the man's face and sat by the body refusing to leave it. The robber, identified as John O'Hara, was buried in St Nicolas' churchyard.

There are great views over the Downs and Lancing College from the drinking area at the front of the pub. In addition to serving good value food they have Harvey's Sussex Best Bitter on hand pump plus four other changing beers from local microbreweries.

*Approximate value today of £60.

** The house, which is a ruin now, features in George Moore's 1894 novel *Esther Walters*.

Left: Displayed on the walls in the upper dining room is an interesting gallery of local photographs.

Right: Marlipins in Old Shoreham High Street dates from the early twelfth century and is one of the oldest surviving secular buildings in Sussex. Through the medieval period it served as a general toll or customs house for the market and port of Shoreham.

Previous: Anyone visiting this old smugglers' haunt today would easily recognise it from R. Thurston Hopkins' 1927 description.

ROTTINGDEAN
The Black Horse

65 High Street Rottingdean, Brighton BN2 7HE

Tel: 01273 300491

Once partly a forge, The Black Horse Inn was a rendezvous for local smugglers.

Rottingdean, a couple of miles east of Brighton, still retains a village feel and is often the subject of picture postcards. The historic centre has a green and pond together with a number of important buildings linked to the smuggling era. The high street leads directly down to the beach dominated on one side by a towering cliff. Although the majority of Rottingdean's inhabitants were families of poorly paid fishermen and agricultural labourers some of the smarter houses in the village are suggestive of an alternative source of income for a privileged few.

The bailiff on the Stanmer Estate, due north of Rottingdean, was one of the smuggling organisers. There were contraband depots in woods behind Stanmer House and the Stanmer chaplain was injured returning from a smuggling run at Rottingdean.

We have seen in an earlier chapter how Brighton developed from the impoverished fishing village of Brighthelmston following The Prince of Wales establishing his Court there in 1783. At that time Brighthelmston and Rottingdean would have been similar in size and the majority of the inhabitants of both were reliant on smuggling to alleviate the wretched social conditions.

During the Regency era the presence of royalty attracted fashionable visitors to the area creating a lively market for luxuries but, as a result, Brighton became too popular for easy landings of goods on the town's beaches. Meanwhile smugglers in the small isolated rural village of Rottingdean enjoyed a boost in demand for their contraband goods from the Prince's extended entourage.

The pub's association with free trading was well known locally and acknowledged today with the 'Smugglers Bar' on the left hand side.

Between the main rooms at the front is a delightful small snug with some matchboard panelling and an old bench seat.

Left: The High Street leads directly down to the beach which is dominated on one side by a towering cliff.

Right: Dating from 1780, the former Custom House in the High Street is the least changed among properties in the village.

The Rottingdean smugglers experienced an obstacle in 1780 with the establishment of a strategically positioned Custom House towards the sea end of the High Street. Any goods (legitimate or otherwise) landed on the beach had to pass the Custom House on the direct route up to the village centre. One way round this was to land contraband at Peacehaven, sometimes even hauling goods up Telescombe Cliffs by means of a horse-powered windlass.

A diary of 1814 refers to 'Captain Dunk', the village butcher who lived at Whipping Post House and could afford to pay

Whipping Post House was home to the village butcher 'Captain Dunk', leader of the smuggling gang.

a custom's fine of £500 although ten of his companions who could not were locked up in Horsham Gaol. It's ironic this old villain lived in front of the whipping post, stocks and ducking stool where other local miscreants were punished for minor misdemeanours.

The interestingly named smuggler Lot Elphic owned several fishing boats and was said to use Rottingdean Windmill as one of his contraband hiding places. At one time the mill's sails were used to signal when the coast was clear for landings. Appearing in photographs in 1890, another local character 'Trunky' Thomas, was one of the last of the village's free traders. He also owned some fishing boats plus four bathing machines and a few cows.

Dr Thomas Hooker's bust is mounted behind the pulpit in St Margaret's church. He was a skilled horseman and acted as a lookout for the Rottingdean smugglers.

The famous educator Dr Thomas Hooker was vicar of Rottingdean from 1792 through forty-six turbulent years of smuggling conflict. He was one of a number of good intentioned churchmen who took the side of their impoverished parishioners against what many considered unjust laws. Hooker, whose bust can be seen behind the pulpit in St Margaret's parish church was a skilled horseman and acted as a lookout for the local smugglers.

The Grange, now a public library, art gallery and museum was formerly Thomas Hooker's rectory, complete with spacious cellars and rumours of a tunnel leading to the beach.

The Elms, an
eighteenth-
century house
facing the village
pond was rented
by Rudyard Kipling
from 1897 to
1903. In 1986
its large garden
was saved from
development
by Rottingdean
Preservation
Society and is now
open to the public.

In 1824 the Newhaven to Brighton road was turnpiked and fifty years later the artistic and literary world began discovering Rottingdean. Sir Edward Burne-Jones came to live at North End House where Rudyard Kipling stayed with his aunt in 1882. Kipling later returned to live at The Elms from 1897 to 1903. Some of the old time smugglers were

This replica of
Kipling's study
is one of the
features in the
Grange Museum
and Art Gallery.

still alive and their reminiscences contributed to Kipling's definitive evocation of the free trading era: *A Smugglers' Song*.

Rottingdean's oldest pub, was built c1513 in the reign of Henry VIII and has been occupying this High Street site ever since. Known locally as 'The Black', it is the oldest entire building in Rottingdean. Part of the pub was formerly a blacksmiths' shop with the forge located in what is now the lounge.

This ancient hostelry's association with free trading was well known locally and acknowledged today with the 'Smugglers Bar' on the left hand side. Between the main rooms at the front is a delightful small snug with some matchboard panelling and an old bench seat.

The interestingly named smuggler Lot Elphic was said to use Rottingdean Windmill as one of his contraband hiding places. At one time the mill's sails were used to signal when the coast was clear for landings.

At The Black Horse today they offer a good range of drinks including local ales and a choice of over 20 gins! The varied menu includes pub classics and gastro dishes, home-made with fresh, locally sourced produce. There is also a great choice of roast lunches on Sundays.

The bailiff on the Stanmer Estate, due north of Rottingdean, was one of the smuggling organisers. There were contraband depots in woods behind Stanmer House and the Stanmer chaplain was injured returning from a smuggling run at Rottingdean.

This former old
country local and
smugglers' haunt
is thought to date
from the sixteenth
century.

SIDLESHAM

The Crab & Lobster

Mill Lane, Sidlesham PO20 7NB

Tel: 01243 641233

Sidlesham lies on one side of Pagham Harbour, the most easterly of the inlets in the Chichester area. Today it is choked with mud and weeds but in the eighteenth century it was still a working port with channels to the quayside both at Sidlesham and Pagham. The silted harbour is now a beautiful nature reserve.

During the days of free traders beaches along the Selsey Bill promontory provided secluded contraband landing sites. The tidal race through the narrow entrance created sufficient current for rafts formed of tubs roped together to be floated through the inlet into the sheltered haven unaided and usually unnoticed. This technique was also used to great

advantage a little further west across the Hampshire border at Langstone and Emsworth.

When vessels brought contraband into Pagham Harbour, it was a simple matter for accomplices on shore to pinpoint the Preventive forces, so goods could be landed on the distant side; crossing the three-quarter mile wide harbour in a boat was far quicker than negotiating the 5 mile circumference on horseback. In 1830 Smugglers made good use of this topographical advantage, luring Revenue Officers to Sidlesham with a decoy light, then landing 700 tubs from a galley at Pagham.

Left: Walkers and bird-watchers are welcome in the small flagstoned bar where light meals are served.

Right: Good imaginative food served in the stylish restaurant includes excellent local fish dishes.

17 wines (including champagne) are available by the glass.

Although the creeks are unnavigable today, some sense of former days can easily be imagined. The row of attractive old buildings still standing close enough to Pagham quayside would certainly have made a convenient temporary hiding place for contraband. At Church Norton, west of the harbour, you can see the remains of a church once linked by a tunnel to the old rectory.

Real ales are from small specialist craft breweries.

On 16 November 1826 an affidavit of Samuel Budd, a quartermaster, employed in the Blockade Station off Pagham, referred to smugglers Thomas Caiger, Daniel Algood, Edward Ticold and John Todd. There was also a Note of Evidence given by Charles Grant which attempts to explain the noise of gunfire. Grant said there was a wedding in Sidlesham: 'and that it is usual when persons of respectability marry to fire off guns by way of rejoicing'. The priest officiating at the wedding would have been smuggling sympathiser Reverend Edward Henry Emillius Goddard, incumbent here from 1823 until 1849.

With the defeat of Napoleon in 1815 the British Government was faced with large numbers of servicemen returning home to poor rural areas. The effect was twofold: more soldiers and sailors were available to confront the domestic smuggling crises but other impoverished men without employment turned to smuggling to support themselves and their families. There was insurrection in the air. By 1824 the Admiralty established the Royal Naval Coast Blockade Service, with a 'Blockade Line' manned by 3000 officers and men, stretching 200 miles along the shores from Sheerness in North Kent round to Chichester.

Reverend Goddard was well aware how a small smuggling supplement to the wages of a poor agricultural labourer or fisherman could make the difference in keeping him and his family from the workhouse. Lieutenant Wilson was a harsh disciplinarian and one of the new officers of the Royal Navy's Coast Blockade whose prime motive was to earn prize money from captured contraband and smuggling vessels.

Children are welcome at tables on the back terrace overlooking the marsh.

In 1828 Wilson declared that Reverend Goddard was openly hostile towards the Preventive men and took every opportunity to defend his parishioners vigorously against any wicked accusations that they were smuggling. He reported that Goddard has: '...interfered with the duty of our officers on several occasions, for example taking the part of a notorious smuggler and the Reverend shows every disposition to encourage litigation in opposition to established laws laid down for the prevention of smuggling'.

The Old Malt House, dating from 1738, stands directly across the lane from the pub.

There is a legend of a civil war skirmish here on the quayside at Sidlesham between Cavaliers and Roundheads. All but one of the Cavaliers were killed with the survivor escaping into the inn. The King's man was later discovered by Cromwell's troopers and unceremoniously despatched.

This former old country local and smugglers' haunt is thought to date from the sixteenth century. Today it is predominantly an upmarket restaurant with rooms although it still functions as a pub and walkers and bird-watchers are welcome in the small flagstoned bar where light meals are served. Real ales are from small specialist craft breweries.

Seventeen wines (including champagne) are available by the glass in the stylish restaurant where good imaginative food

includes excellent local fish dishes. The garden looks out over the bird reserve of silted Pagham Harbour and children are welcome at tables on the back terrace overlooking the marsh.

The pub garden looks out over Sidlesham's silted harbour which is now a beautiful nature reserve.

Reverend Goddard, incumbent at St Mary Our Lady parish church from 1823 until 1849, was openly hostile towards Preventive men and took every opportunity to defend his parishioners vigorously against any wicked accusations that they were smuggling.

The brick and flint pub was formerly three cottages linked together in 1668 to form one dwelling.

STEYNING
The Norfolk Arms

18 Church Street, Steyning BN44 3YB

Tel: 01903 812215

In addition to the ancient front door there is a Jacobean studded door off the right hand rear room inscribed '1668 RW' referring to Richard White (owner at that time).

Steyning's impressive main street is rich in old houses from the fifteenth, sixteenth and seventeenth centuries featuring stone roofs, mullioned windows and overhanging storeys but the best is yet to come. Church Street is one of the finest streets in Sussex.

It begins with the fifteenth-century Brotherhood Hall which became a school for fifty pupils during Shakespeare's later life. From the hall ancient timber-framed houses rub shoulders one with another as the road inclines towards the

The lounge bar was originally two small rooms, the rear area comprising part of the landlord's accommodation until 1935.

The Norfolk Arms serves three changing beers in addition to the resident Harvey's Sussex Best Bitter.

church. Here, tight under property eaves, a number of small windows serve as a reminder of the town's smuggling past. This is where candles were placed to alert local free traders of the presence of patrolling Preventive men.

In 1801 a Steyning smuggler named Holden was found guilty of assaulting a Revenue Officer, whilst engaged in 'running' smuggled goods. A witness statement at his trial detailed the following events which led to his conviction.

Original beams are evident as are real open fires.

Samuel Jones, the Supervisor of Excise at Steyning reported he was returning home one night between ten and eleven with another officer named John Orchard, when he heard the noise of a number of horses. The two men stopped in a lane and Orchard went over into a field. A party of smugglers consisting of 16 or so men came up the lane. Three of them were light (that is to say their horses were not carrying goods), the remaining horses appeared to have tubs slung over them... the three light men advanced towards the witness.

One of these men, named Meeting, exclaimed 'Damn you, what do you do here?' Thinking he recognized one of the men Jones said 'Mr Chandler is that you?' Whereupon Meeting, Holden and Chandler struck him with very heavy sticks almost knocking him off his horse.

Jones's arm was beaten as black as his hat and as he was retreating he received a very severe blow on the back of his head. He almost fell but managed to spur his horse and got away. He was prevented from making the seizure owing to the violent treatment he received. Interestingly his colleague

Tight under cottage eaves along Church Street are a number of small windows where candles were placed to alert local free traders of the presence of patrolling preventive men.

Orchard, does not get a mention after his craven escape into a field.

* * *

Over three decades later, on Tuesday, 22 February 1832, Steyning's most remembered smuggler William Cowerson was killed. The incident happened during the most notorious local contraband run, known today as: The Battle of Worthing High Street.

The thirty-one-year-old stonemason is thought to have lived in what is now 'Smugglers' Cottage' in Steyning. A sword displayed in Steyning Museum was discovered under the thatch when the cottage roof was repaired. Cowerson's day job involved restoration work on the tower of Tarring church and he is thought to have hidden contraband in various places including tombs in the churchyard.

He must have been a big man because an oversize grave was required to receive his body. At his passing the church bell

William Cowerson is thought to have lived in what is now 'Smuggler's Cottage' in Steyning.

tolled for four hours, reported in a local newspaper as: 'a merry peal'. The young smuggler was well respected in the town and his hero's burial was very well attended. A fellow artisan described him as: 'As fine a fellow and thorough Englishman as ever lived'. His expensive ornate gravestone can still be seen in Steyning churchyard. The epitaph makes no mention of the fact he lost his life while fighting against the lawful forces of his country. It reads:

'Death with his dart doth pierce my heart
When I was in my prime.
Grieve not for me my dearest friends
For it was God's appointed time.
Our life hangs by a single thread
Which soon is cut and we are dead,
Therefore repent, make no delay,
For in my bloom I was called away.'

The Norfolk Arms is a real gem situated just about halfway down Church Street directly opposite a terrace of former smugglers' cottages. It is a traditional relaxed beer drinkers' pub with flexible opening hours. As you enter you step back in time for this is as unpretentious a village tavern as you

Cowerson's body was buried here in Steyning churchyard with no hint on his gravestone's inscription of how he met his end.

are likely to see with an ambience that is welcoming and friendly. When Cowerson and his free trading friends met here it was one of the town's numerous unlicensed drinking dens and did not become an official ale house until 1880.

The brick and flint pub was formerly three cottages linked together in 1668 to form one dwelling. The right hand cottage was once a bakery. The lounge bar on the right was originally two small rooms, the rear area comprised part of the landlord's accommodation until 1935. Look for the Jacobean studded door off the right hand rear room inscribed '1668 RW' referring to Richard White (owner at that time). The listed description includes reference to a 'good 17th century staircase'. Toilets were not added until the 1930s!

The Battle of Worthing High Street

Two hours after midnight on 22 February 1832, a boat carrying 300 tubs of contraband spirits became beached on the sands on Worthing's seafront. It was bright moonlight and two hundred smugglers, bodyguards and assistants began unloading the cargo which included perfume, in addition to French brandy and Dutch gin. The landing party consisted of 200 local tub men flanked by 50 'batmen' said to be from Bexhill carrying clubs and staves.

Unfortunately for the smugglers the moonlight allowed a coastguard at East Worthing to spot the convoy and his alarm flare quickly brought out a force led by Lieutenant Henderson of the Royal Navy's Coast Blockade. By then the gang had managed to unload 250 tubs. Although they heavily outnumbered the preventive men, and despite the presence of the 50 batmen, most of the smugglers took to their heels.

Henderson quickly marshalled his troops and a running battle soon ensued along the High Street and surrounding lanes, where smugglers had begun to dissipate. In Warwick

An English **Small-Sword**
from about 1690-1720

It was found in the thatch of "Smuggler",
Church Street when the thatch was being
removed and replaced with tiles in the
1920's.

Could the thatch have been used to hide
the sword from the Excise men? There is
no way of knowing.

This sword displayed in Steyning Museum was discovered under the thatch of Smuggler's Cottage when the roof was repaired.

Street, some residents opened their doors to allow the free traders to escape through to the rear streets.

While mounted officers galloped through the lanes firing pistols, smugglers made off with numerous kegs. More than thirty minders managed to keep the Blockade men at bay until the smugglers reached a narrow footbridge crossing the Teville Stream on the outskirts of town. Unfortunately the bridge gate was locked forcing the free traders to turn and fight.

Lieutenant Henderson cocked his pistols and ordered the desperate men to surrender but Cowerson struck with his bludgeon breaking the officer's arm. Undaunted, the Lieutenant raised his other pistol and shot Cowerson dead. The jury at the Coroner's Inquest held in the nearby Anchor Inn decided the killing was justified. Cowerson's body was buried in Steyning churchyard with no hint on his gravestone's inscription of how he met his end.

WEST TARRING
The George & Dragon
1 High Street, Tarring, Worthing BN14 7NN
Tel: 01903 202497

The pub sign hangs up rather than down because until recently double-decker buses ran a regular service past the pub along the narrow High Street in both directions.

The village of Tarring is now a suburb of Worthing but was once one of the most important market towns in this part of West Sussex with origins dating from Saxon times. It still retains a number of historic buildings around the village centre. Smuggling miller John Oliver of Highdown owned property in Worthing and The Hollies in Tarring's narrow High Street.

In 1601 The Hollies was owned by the vicar John Evans. The house passed through a number of owners before being bought by Richard Hedgecock in 1774. He undertook extensive modernisation including facing the timber-frame building with brick and flint. To cover the cost of the renovations Hedgecock took out a mortgage on the property for £160 at 4% from John Oliver and, finally in 1778, sold

The George, or 'G&D' as it is known locally, is a bit of a time capsule with original brick and flint walls and dark wooden beams.

The Hollies to him. Although the house was then owned by Oliver, Mariah Hedgecock continued to live there and, on the miller's death in 1793, it was inherited by Mariah's eighteen-year-old son John Oliver Hedgecock. From this it seems likely that Mariah was the miller's daughter and John Oliver Hedgecock was his grandson.

Worthing and Goring beaches were regularly used by free traders from the villages of Durrington, Salvington, Broadwater, Sompting and (above all) West Tarring who were enthusiastic participants in the smuggling trade.

There are persistent stories linking the men of Tarring and The George & Dragon in particular with smuggling. In 1860 the vicar of Tarring confirmed this when he wrote: 'They were used to say here, that every other man you met was a smuggler – but it was a mild, soft sort of speech, for, in truth, there was no man, who, one way or another, was not concerned in some venture or another.'

During the turbulent Coast Blockade period (1817–31) there were running street battles in West Sussex towns between smugglers and Preventive men. Around 10pm on 25 March 1827, Lieutenant Henry Leworthy of West Worthing Station was in action when he and his men encountered a large gang of smugglers near Tarring Road. About 30 armed men and perhaps 200 others, '...many with bludgeons 4 to 5 feet long...' were gathering for a landing and the appearance of the Blockade Party brought brisk volleys of fire from the smugglers. Lieutenant Peake and his men from another station then arrived and the firing continued for five minutes or more from both sides. The smugglers then scattered but 39 were reported to have taken refuge in The George & Dragon at Tarring.

Leworthy placed a cordon of men around the pub to prevent anyone escaping and rode to the residence of the only

The G&D is a beer drinkers' pub, well supported by regular local clientele.

On entering the old hostelry, you are greeted by the singular long bar and the undeniable feeling of being in a real pub.

The bar area with its impressive range of real ales is illuminated by a rare 1970s Watney's sign.

available magistrate to obtain a search warrant – but to his chagrin the justice was not home! Left with no alternative the Lieutenant was forced to lift the cordon. He was however able to report no contraband was landed that night and one smuggler had been shot dead and another badly wounded. For once no injuries were sustained by any of his men.

The varying floor levels indicate development and extension over many years.

In 1597 Sir Walter Raleigh granted a licence 'to sell wines retail' to Walter Crabbe of Tarring and it seems likely Crabbe's business premises occupied the site of the present George & Dragon. Certainly Moses Brian owned a tavern here called The White Horse in 1610. The pub continued to trade as The White Horse with the first reference to its present name appearing in 1855.

Known locally as the G&D this ancient hostelry spent a period as a coaching inn before the development of Worthing in the early nineteenth century. A pencil drawing by Sarah Winton Hide dated 1869 shows the pub with a two-storey

Left: Smuggling miller John Oliver of Highdown owned property in Worthing plus The Hollies further up Tarring High Street, on the other side of the road from the pub.

Right: A fast turnaround for passengers and horses was essential for coaching inns. The 1869 drawing shows the addition of a two-storey bay window extension.

Opposite: Smuggler William Cowerson's day job as a stonemason involved him in repairs to the tower of St Andrew's parish church, a short walk from the pub.

bay window extension which G&D staff used to keep an eye out for approaching stagecoaches. Sarah was the daughter of Charles Winton listed as 'landlord and butcher' who was in charge from 1855 until Sarah's husband Mark Hide took over in 1878.

This traditional locals' pub has oak beams throughout and a choice of several split-level seating areas, including a cosy lounge with a coal-effect fire. Darts are played here and a beer festival is held in April, around St George's Day. The pub inside is a bit of a time capsule with original brick and flint walls and an abundance of dark wooden beams. The varying floor levels indicate development and extension over many years and during building work in 1967 a 22ft well was discovered under the kitchen floor.

On entering the pub, you are greeted by the singular long bar with a recessed 'sports' bar (no pool table, just a dart board). There is a rear dining room on the right and a cosy little tucked away corner. The back door leads out to an enclosed rear garden divided into three sections with suntrap patio. The pub sign hangs up rather than down because until recently double-decker buses ran a regular service past the pub in both directions along the narrow High Street.

EPILOGUE
Fear & Greed

Smuggling began around 1700 with small local enterprises driven by need. Within fifty years it had evolved into organised crime on a massive scale fuelled by greed. Smugglers did not have the exclusivity on greed, leaders among Preventive men were also avaricious. Officers in Customs and Excise and the armed services received 'prize money' for seizures of contraband. In theory, a percentage of rewards filtered down through the ranks but in a classic stick and carrot scenario ordinary soldiers and sailors were also incentivized to duty by the threat of the lash.

James William McCulloch, Captain of H.M.S. *Severn*, is acknowledged as creator of the 'Royal Navy Coast Blockade Service for the Prevention of Smuggling'. McCulloch was a harsh disciplinarian to the point of cruelty and known by his men as 'Flogging Joey'. In the Blockade Service weekly punishment took place on the open deck of a ship in the presence of the Captain, the officers and both watches of the crew on special muster.

The offender, having been held below in irons, was brought on deck stripped to the waist and tied to a vertical grating. After the Captain had read aloud the offence and punishment a Bosun's Mate, would flog the prisoner with a cat-o-nine-tails. The petty officer would exert full strength at full stretch, knowing he dare not ease up. In addition to the usual punishments for drunkenness, desertion and disobedience, extracts from McCulloch's ship's log interestingly listed penalties for being bribed 24 lashes; found in a smuggler's house 36 and corrupt conduct 40.

The smugglers' lash of choice was a horsewhip, wielded to deadly effect on despised informers and even those suspected

The Hawkhurst Gang was a notorious criminal organisation involved in smuggling throughout southeast England.

of the crime. In 1778 a club-footed breeches maker named Clumpy Bowles from Leiston in Suffolk turned informer. He was whipped and left for dead by smugglers Tom Tiberton and Nosey Debney but survived to give evidence against them. In December 1782, in Thornham Village Norfolk, Excise Officer Robert Bliss lost the sight in one eye when attacked with a lead-tipped whip whilst trying to arrest a smuggler called William Franklyn.

West Sussex was the setting for two of the most horrific tales in the history of smuggling, both involving whipping. These sadistic attacks had the effect of completely changing public perception towards smugglers. Formerly they had been seen as friendly Robin Hood type characters but subsequently were recognised as gangsters who frequently terrorised their own neighbourhoods. The barbaric incidents recounted here led to a public outcry and the ultimate destruction of the big eighteenth-century gangs. These events also demonstrate how pubs played an integral role in smugglers' lives.

The former Dog & Partridge alehouse where Richard Hawkins was savagely murdered was located at Slindon Common in West Sussex.

The Dog & Partridge Alehouse

Both brutal stories feature members of the notorious Kent based gang from Hawkhurst who established a safe but seditious sanctuary in The Oak & Ivy pub. They operated across southern England from Deal to Portsmouth. The first incident centred on the West Sussex village of Slindon and the former Dog & Partridge alehouse. Sometime in the early 1740s Jeremiah 'Butler' Curtis, a butcher who had been part of a violent gang from Hastings, joined forces with the Hawkhurst Gang and proved to be one of its most vicious members.

In January 1748 Richard Hawkins, a farm labourer from Yapton, had been threshing corn in a barn at Walberton where members of the Hawkhurst Gang had hidden 12 parcels of tea. Curtis and another gang member, John 'Smoker' Mills, of Trotton in West Sussex, came to collect the smuggled goods and found two parcels were missing. Assuming Hawkins had taken them they went looking for him. After discovering his whereabouts, they forced him at gunpoint to sit in the saddle of Mills' horse. The smugglers

Smugglers John Mills and Richard Rowland whipping Richard Hawkins to death in The Dog & Partridge.

Charles Lennox, 2nd Duke of Richmond, is thought to be the chronicler of these smugglers' tales. However, it is clear from this drawing, that neither the Duke nor his illustrator ever visited the humble Dog & Partridge alehouse.

and their captive rode to The Dog & Partridge alehouse on Slindon Common where Hawkins was tortured and murdered.

According to accounts of the inquest and subsequent trial, Hawkins was forced into the back room of the pub where other members of the gang were waiting. A 'Smugglers' Court' was held with Mills, Curtis, Thomas Winter (a coachman of Polling near Arundel) and Richard Roland alias Robb or 'Little Fat Back', Jeramiah Curtis' servant who lived near East Grinstead. The group assumed the role of Judge and Jury.

To elicit a confession from Hawkins he was punched, kicked and whipped. John Reynolds, landlord of the Dog & Partridge, advised him to confess because it would go easier for him. In an attempt to stop further beatings Hawkins implicated his father-in-law, John Cockrel Senior of Walberton and his brother-in-law also named John Cockrel who was an alehouse keeper in Yapton. A couple of the smugglers broke off from the beatings and left to find these two men and take them prisoner but in their absence Hawkins died of his injuries.

On their return to the pub the two smugglers were confronted with the sorry outcome and became fearful for their necks. They released their prisoners after swearing them to secrecy. The gang members then carted Hawkins body 12 miles to Parham Park, owned by Sir Cecil Bishop. They weighted the corpse with rocks and immersed it in a pond in the park where it remained undiscovered for nine months. During a consequential investigation into the crime a pardon was given to one of the smugglers who had nothing to do with the murder, in return for supplying incriminating evidence.

Captain James William McCulloch of Coastal Blockade Vessel H.M.S. *Severn* was known to his men as 'Flogging Joey'.

Smuggler John Mills and landlord John Reynolds were arrested and tried at East Grinstead Assizes. Curtis by this time had escaped arrest and fled to France. Reynolds was

Members of McCulloch's crew could expect 24 lashes of the cat-o-nine-tails if caught being bribed by a smuggler, 36 if found in a smuggler's house and 40 if found guilty of corrupt conduct.

found not guilty of murder but later tried, along with his wife, for withholding information. Mills, aged thirty, was found guilty of murder and hung from gallows erected on Slindon Common near the Dog & Partridge. Afterwards his body was hung in chains from a gibbet as an example to other would be murderers. Hawkins left behind a wife and many children. On a further search of the barn, the missing tea was discovered where it had been previously overlooked.

The right hand side of the building, seen here from the rear, was part of the original Dog & Partridge alehouse.

The former Dog & Partridge alehouse on Slindon Common is now two private cottages.

Opposite page: It was here where smugglers John Mills and Richard Rowland savagely murdered Richard Hawkins. (Photographs curtesy of Jan Trott.)

The Old Forge in Reynolds' Lane, has been successfully converted into a local Shop and Café. It opened in October 2012 and the volunteers commissioned a range of ales to commemorate the lost pubs of Slindon. However, the information on the Dog & Partridge label is somewhat misleading. As you can see from Jan Trott's photographs the building was not demolished in the 1950s.

Barbarous Usage

This is a story of two journeys. On the first leg we visit the locations of Charlton Forest, the former White Hart Inn at Rowland's Castle, The Custom House at Poole and The George Inn at Fordingbridge. The second stage begins back at the White Hart and follows the West Sussex/Hampshire border 5 miles north to Lady Holt Park; then a further 7 miles to the village of Rake and the former Red Lion. As we follow these trails events unfold like the plot of a horror film.

For John 'Smoker' Mills, torture and violence was clearly a way of life. He was part of a group who, less than a fortnight after the slaying of Richard Hawkins at the Dog & Partridge, committed two even more grisly murders. This story however has its origins in events that occurred four months earlier in September 1747. It begins with a smuggling venture organised by two groups acting in concert: the Hawkhurst Gang whom we have already met and a group from Dorset.

Smugglers' representative Richard Perrin from Chichester, sailed to Guernsey on a Rye boat, commissioned to buy about 2 tons of tea and 30 casks of brandy. The goods were duly loaded and the vessel embarked on the return voyage to a planned rendezvous near Lymington in Christchurch Bay. Things went awry mid-channel on 22 September when the smuggling lugger was overtaken by the Revenue cutter Swift, commanded by Captain William Johnson. The contraband was seized and taken to a government warehouse in Poole, the crew having escaped in a small boat.

The principal sponsors of the venture were naturally dismayed and at a meeting in Charlton Forest of sixty interested parties, Perrin made an agreement to recover the contraband. On 5 October, thirty armed smugglers met at Rowland's Castle in The White Hart Inn owned and run by a family in league with the smugglers.

During the course of the following day the gang rode to Poole, arriving about 11 pm, when they immediately encountered a problem because the Custom House was protected by the guns of a naval sloop. The Dorset men wanted to abandon the enterprise but whilst they argued the falling tide put the Custom House out of sight of the battleship and the raid was able to go ahead according to plan. Two members of the gang, using crowbars and axes, broke into the warehouse around 2 am on 8 October and everyone worked quickly to load the pack horses.

The smugglers took virtually all the tea but left the brandy, presumably because they had insufficient transport. The heavily laden convoy then set out for Brook in the New Forest, planning to weigh the tea and share it out with each man expecting to receive a little over a hundredweight. As the caravan passed through Fordingbridge it attracted a great deal of attention.

Before crossing the River Avon the outlaws stopped for breakfast at the George Inn.

Galley and Chater
were put together
on a horse, with
their legs tied
under the animal's
belly with Jackson
shouting 'Whip
them, cut them,
slash them, damn
them!'

The George Inn at Fordingbridge

At no point had the outlaws been opposed, and it seems likely they were elated by their success. The mounted smugglers emerged from the inn yard feeling refreshed from their meal and rest when John 'Dimer' Diamond, one of the Hawkhurst Gang, spotted a familiar face in the crowd. It was shoemaker Daniel Chater who Diamond had worked with getting in the late summer harvest. Diamond reached down to shake Daniel's hand and then threw him a small bag of tea.

As the convoy headed off towards the New Forest, Chater chatted innocently to his neighbours in the crowd explaining how he knew Diamond but this was to be his undoing. When the authorities started investigating the Poole raid they heard about the Fordingbridge incident and arrested Diamond on suspicion of his involvement. The collector of customs at Chichester subpoenaed Chater as a potential key witness to positively identify the smuggler.

On Valentine's Day 1748 William Galley, an ageing minor customs official was sent to chaperone the shoemaker on what proved to be a fateful journey. The luckless couple left

After prolonged torture smugglers eventually threw the shoemaker William Chater down a well and stoned him to death.

Southampton heading for the home of a JP near Chichester, carrying a letter with instructions that Chater should go to Chichester Gaol to identify Diamond.

The White Hart Inn at Rowland's Castle

When the pair reached the Hampshire / West Sussex border they lost their way but were guided by a couple of local men as far as the White Hart Inn at Rowland's Castle. This disreputable smugglers' den was an unfortunate place for them to break their journey. The landlady became suspicious of their intentions and sent for William Jackson and William Carter, who lived close by. Galley and Chater wanted to press on but the landlady made an excuse about lost stable keys and delayed the pair just long enough for a group of smugglers to arrive headed by Jackson and Carter. Innocent witnesses were sent away from the pub as the smugglers began to drink heavily. Jackson forcefully persuaded Galley and Chater to drink with them.

Very soon, drowsy with drink, the custom's man and his witness went to sleep in an adjoining room. As they slept, the smugglers crept in and took the letter. The contents plainly spelt out the intentions of the men, and the smugglers held a council of war. Whilst the smugglers continued to drink heavily various proposals were made as what should be done with the prisoners. The most humane suggestion was to send them to France, but two of the smugglers' wives said no punishment was severe enough and egged their husbands on saying: 'Hang the dogs, for they came here to hang us'.

The Torture Begins

When this conference ended, Jackson donned his spurs then woke the sleeping men by climbing on the bed and spurring their foreheads. He then began whipping them, providing a foretaste of the torture to follow. Galley and Chater were taken outside, and put together on a horse, with their legs tied under the animal's belly. They hadn't got more than a hundred yards when Jackson shouted 'Whip them, cut them, slash them, damn them!'

During the following mile five of the smugglers attacked Galley and Chater whipping them so badly they slid sideways on the horse ending up hanging beneath its belly; at each step one or the other was kicked in the head by the horse's hooves. Eventually untied, but now so weak they couldn't sit in a saddle unaided, they were separated, and each sat behind one of the smugglers.

The merciless whipping and beating continued on the long journey with Galley lying prone across his own horse. For half a mile the poor man cried out: 'Barbarous usage, barbarous usage! For God's sake shoot me through the head'. This only provoked Jackson to further cruelty and he began squeezing the prisoner's testicles. As they passed Lady Holt Park, near Harting, there was talk of killing both men and throwing them down Harris's Well but undecided they pressed on for another 7 miles heading for the Red

Lion at Rake north of Rogate. They reached the pub in the early hours of Monday morning, after stopping briefly at the house of another reputed smuggler who '...imagining they were upon some villainous expedition...' refused to help them.

The Red Lion at Rake

Chater the shoemaker was miraculously still capable of standing by the time the miserable rabble reached The Red Lion. He was taken out and chained up in a turf store. Galley, the customs man appeared to be dead and the smugglers temporarily hid his body in the brew-house attached to the pub. Later that night they carried the 'corpse' about three quarters of a mile to Harting Coombe where they enlarged a fox-earth, bundled the old man into the hole and shovelled soil back on top.

When the corpse was found some time later, it was apparent Galley had recovered consciousness after being interred, for he was sitting almost upright and had a hand raised to keep out the dirt out of his nose and eyes.

For the smugglers, there was still the problem of Chater. He remained chained in the turf store for three days too ill to eat. After a meeting on the Wednesday night it was

The former Red Lion at Rake.

Opposite: The Smugglers' Stone was erected in 1749 to record the execution of seven smugglers. It marks the place where three of them (Jackson, Mills senior and Mills junior) were hanged.

resolved he should be murdered and his body dumped in Harris's Well as originally planned. The gang went out to the store and one of them called Tapner, barked an order to the shoemaker: '...down on your knees and go to prayers, for with this knife I will be your butcher.' As Chater knelt, Tapner slashed his face twice, completely cutting through his nose, and virtually blinding him. Eventually the party set off for the well, with the heartless Tapner continuing to whip Chater and threatening him with all manner of tortures if he spilt his own blood on the horse's saddle!

The Guildhall Chichester in the centre of Priory Park where a specially convened Court was held to try members of the Hawkhurst gang.

The Smugglers' Stone

After being apprehended in January 1749, the gang was brought to trial on the 16th at a special Court held in the Guildhall, Chichester; now in the centre of Priory Park. Seven of the members were sentenced to hang the following day on gallows erected in an area of the city called the Broyle. The principal murderers' bodies were then hung in chains

(gibbeted) one on the Portsmouth Road near Rake, two on Selsey Bill, one near Chichester at Rook's Hill and one at Horsmonden in Kent. Gibbeting was usually reserved for murderers and highwaymen. It was an unusual punishment for smugglers but reflected how seriously the authorities took the murderous actions of the Hawkhurst Gang and its associates.

A stone was placed at The Broyle in Chichester marking the location where three of the savage smugglers, Jackson, Mills senior and Mills junior met their fate. At that time the Broyle was a deer-park but the stone has subsequently been moved and now stands outside the field down Broyle Road close to Roussillon Park. The inscription, which is no longer legible read:

> *Near this place was buried the body of William Jackson, a prescribed smuggler, who upon a special commission of oyer and terminer held at Chichester on the 16th day of January 1748-9 was, with William Carter, attained for the murder of William Galley, a custom house officer and who likewise was together with Benjamin Tapner, John Cobby, John Hammond, Richard Mills the elder and Richard Mills the younger, his son, attained for the murder of Daniel Chater. But dying in a few hours after sentence of death was pronounced upon him he thereby escaped the punishment which the heinousness of his complicated crimes deserved and which was the next day most justly inflicted upon his accomplices. As a memorial to posterity and a warning to this and succeeding generations this stone is erected AD 1749.*

With the cruel deaths of Galley and Chater, among others, causing national outrage, the names of known smugglers were published in the *London Gazette*. Any smuggler so listed was instructed to hand themselves in within 40 days of the publication date. In all, at least 75 of the gang were hanged or transported.

BIBLIOGRAPHY

Brigid Chapman: *West Sussex Inns*

Bob Copper: *Across Sussex with Belloc*

Roger Davies: *Tarring – A Walk Through its History*

Trevor May: *Smugglers and Smuggling*

Roy Philp: *The Coast Blockade*
The Royal Navy's War on Smuggling in Kent & Sussex 1817 - 31

David Phillipson: *Smuggling – A History 1700 - 1970*

Richard Platt: *The Ordnance Survey Guide to Smuggler's Britain*

Donald Stuart: *Old Sussex Inns*

Mary Waugh: *Smuggling in Kent & Sussex 1700 – 1840*